# Colours in Nature

# Red

Lisa Bruce

**Heinemann**
LIBRARY

Little Nippers

**www.heinemann.co.uk/library**
Visit our website to find out more information about **Heinemann Library** books.

To order:
☎ Phone 44 (0) 1865 888066
🖹 Send a fax to 44 (0) 1865 314091
💻 Visit the Heinemann Bookshop at www.heinemann.co.uk/library to browse our catalogue and order online.

First published in Great Britain by Heinemann Library, Halley Court, Jordan Hill, Oxford OX2 8EJ, part of Harcourt Education. Heinemann is a registered trademark of Harcourt Education Ltd.

Editorial: Jilly Attwood and Claire Throp
Design: Jo Hinton-Malivoire and bigtop, Bicester, UK
Models made by: Jo Brooker
Picture Research: Catherine Bevan
Production: Séverine Ribierre

Originated by Dot Gradations
Printed and bound in China by South China Printing Company

ISBN 0 431 17230 7 (hardback)
07 06 05 04 03
10 9 8 7 6 5 4 3 2 1

ISBN 0 431 17235 8 (paperback)
07 06 05 04 03
10 9 8 7 6 5 4 3 2 1

**British Library Cataloguing in Publication Data**
Bruce, Lisa
Red – (Colours in nature)
535.6
A full catalogue record for this book is available from the British Library.

**Acknowledgements**
The publishers would like to thank the following for permission to reproduce photographs:
Ardea pp. **8-9** (J. A. Bailey), **12** (Dennis Avon); Bruce Coleman (Jim Watt) pp. **4-5**, (Andrew Purcell) **16-17**; Corbis p. **19**; Garden Matters pp. **22** (Sheila Apps), **23** (Colin Milkins); KPT Power Photos pp. **7** (left), **20-21**; NHPA p. **7** (right) (G. I. Bernard); Photodisc pp. **6**, **10-11**, **13** , **14-15**, **15** (inset), **18**

Cover photograph reproduced with permission of Photodisc

The publishers would like to thank Annie Davy for her assistance in the preparation of this book.

Every effort has been made to contact copyright holders of any material reproduced in this book. Any omissions will be rectified in subsequent printings if notice is given to the publishers.

# Contents

Red in nature.

Nature is full of wonderful colours.

What can you think of in nature that is red?

# Red food

Red pepper

Do you like to eat any of these red foods?

Red for danger

These red toadstools mean DANGER.

8

You would get very sick if you ate them.

9

# Red in autumn

In autumn the leaves on some trees change colour.

They turn from green to red and then fall off.

# Red in winter

tweet

tweet

In winter a robin's red breast stands out against the snow.

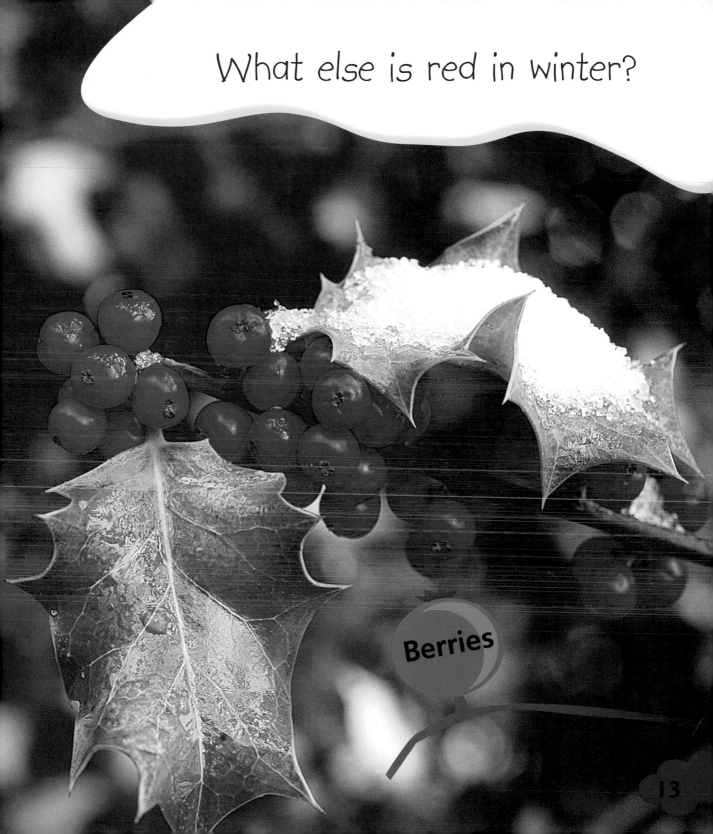

What else is red in winter?

Berries

# Red flowers

These poppies
are scarlet red.

This rose is a dark red called crimson.

15

# Red insects

This red ladybird has black spots.

How many spots can you count?

# Red rocks

In some places rocks are red.

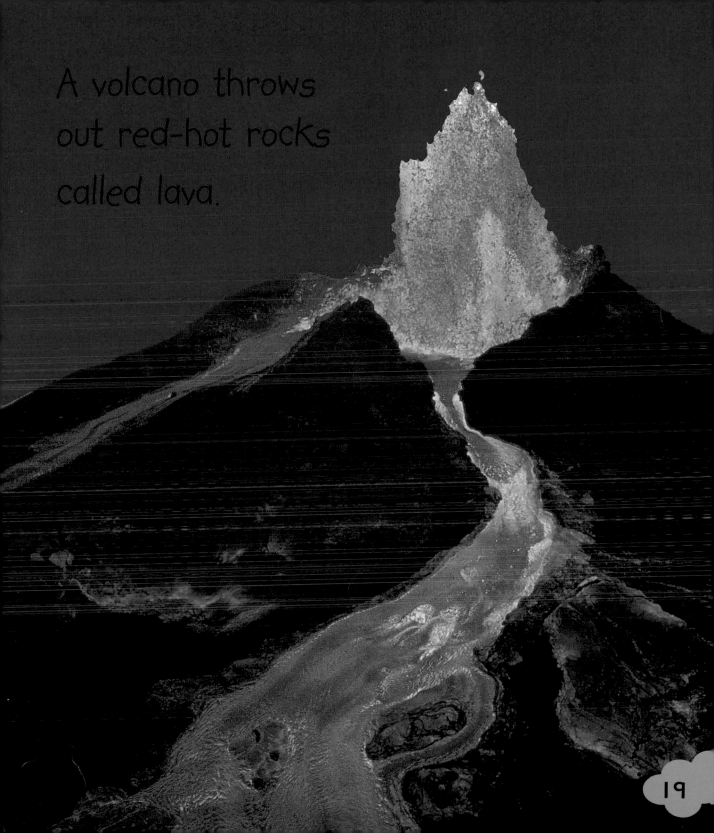

A volcano throws
out red-hot rocks
called lava.

19

# Red sky

Sometimes the sky can look red.

Red in the morning is called sunrise.

When
the sky is red
in the evening it is
a sunset.

# Changing colour

When fruit ripens it changes colour.

These strawberries are green.

When they are ripe they turn red and you can eat them.

# Index

The end

## Notes for adults

This series supports young children's knowledge and understanding of the world around them. The four books will help to form the foundation for later work in science and geography. The following Early Learning Goals are relevant to this series:

- begin to differentiate colours
- explore what happens when they mix colours
- find out about and identify some features of living things, objects and events they observe
- look closely at similarities, differences, patterns and change
- ask questions about why things happen and how things work
- observe, find out about and identify features in the places they live and the natural world
- find out about their environment, and talk about those features they like and dislike

The *Colours in Nature* series introduces children to colours and their different shades by exploring features of the natural world. It will also help children to think more about living things and life processes, which may lead on to discussion of environmental issues. The children should be encouraged to be aware of the weather and seasonal changes and how these affect the place in which they live.

This book will help children extend their vocabulary, as they will hear new words such as pepper, toadstool, scarlet, crimson, volcano, lava and ripens.

### Additional information

Ladybirds are insects as they have six legs and a body divided into three parts. Ladybirds cannot hear but can feel vibrations with their feet. They are also able to squirt a bitter liquid at an attacker. Ayers rock (page 18) is also known by its Aboriginal name Uluru, which means 'great pebble'. Out of every 10,000 eggs that a female lobster releases only 1% may survive. Lobsters have the ability to regenerate parts of their body. For example, if they lose a claw in a fight they can grow another one.

### Follow-up activities

Using red paint, make a collage of thumbprints. Add a beak and feet to turn them into robins. The children could colour in branches for the birds to sit on.

Sing nursery rhymes with a red theme such as 'Ladybird, Ladybird fly away home' and 'Ring-a-Ring of Roses'.